NICKELODEON

SpongeBob squarepants™

MERMAID TO MEASURE

TITAN BOOKS

SPONGEBOB SQUAREPANTS: MERMAID TO MEASURE

ISBN 1 84576 224 X
ISBN-13 9781845762247

Stories & Scripts: C.H. Greenblatt, Sherm Cohen, Jay Lender, Sam Henderson, Derek
Drymon, Mark Crilley, David Lewman, Graham Annable, James Kochalka, Kaz
Pencils & Inks: C.H. Greenblatt, Sherm Cohen, Jay Lender, Ted Couldron, Jeff
Albrecht, Greg Schigiel, Graham Annable, Vince Deporter
Colours: Sno Cone Studios, Digital Chameleon, Stu Chaifetz
Letters: C.H. Greenblatt, Sherm Cohen, Jay Lender, Comicraft, Graham Annable
Photo Panels: Nick Jennings
Photos: Stefanie Scholler, Jeremy Henderson

Published by Titan Books,
a division of Titan Publishing Group Ltd.
144 Southwark St
London SE1 0UP

A CIP catalogue record for this title is available from the British Library.

This edition first published: September 2006

3 5 7 9 10 8 6 4

Printed in Italy.

Also available from Titan:
SpongeBob SquarePants: Gone Jelly Fishing (ISBN: 1 84576 223 1)
Star Wars Clone Wars Adventures Vol. 1 (ISBN: 1 84023 995 6)
Star Wars Clone Wars Adventures Vol. 2 (ISBN: 1 84023 840 2)
Star Wars Clone Wars Adventures Vol. 3 (ISBN: 1 84576 020 4)
Star Wars Clone Wars Adventures Vol. 4 (ISBN: 1 84576 189 8)
Star Wars Clone Wars Adventures Vol. 5 (ISBN: 1 84576 275 4)

What did you think of this book? We love to hear from our readers. Please email us at:
readerfeedback@titanemail.com, or write to us at the above address. You can also
visit us at www.titanbooks.com

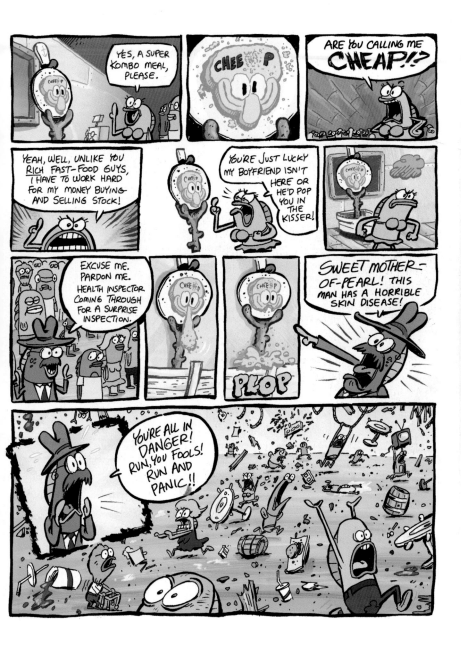

The End

Story: Sam Henderson. Pencils and inks: Vince Deporter. Coloring: Stu Chaifetz. Editor: Dave Roman. *SpongeBob SquarePants* created by Steve Hillenburg.

Nicktoons Special

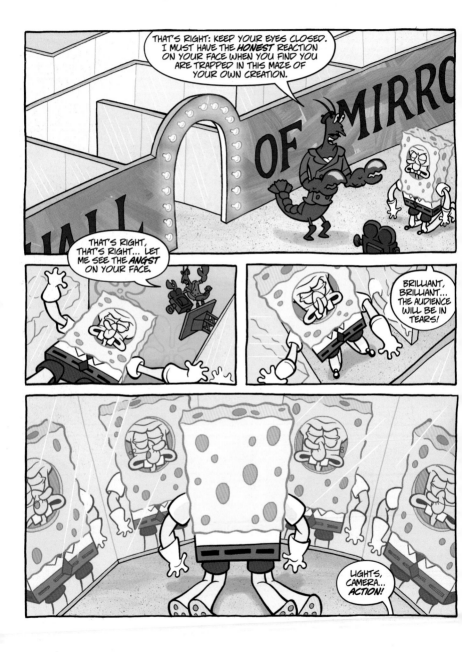

Plot: Sam Henderson. Script, pencils, and inks: Joy Lender. Coloring: Digital Chameleon. Lettering: Sherm Cohen. SpongeBob SquarePants created by Stephen Hillenburg.

STORY DAVID LEWMAN · PENCILS GREGG SCHIGIEL · INKS JEFF ALBRECHT · COLOR SNO CONE STUDIOS · LETTERS COMICRAFT

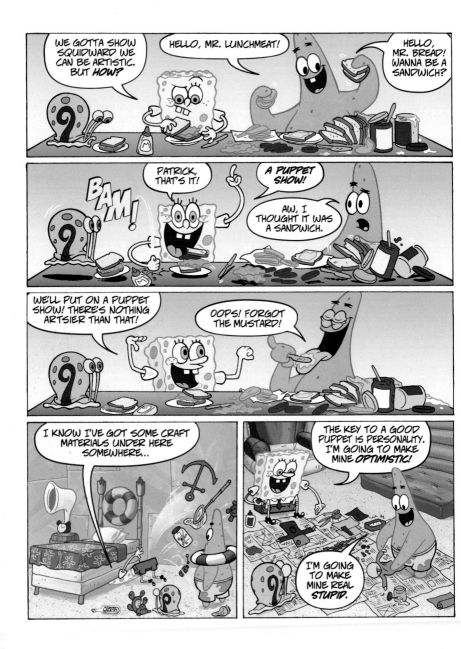

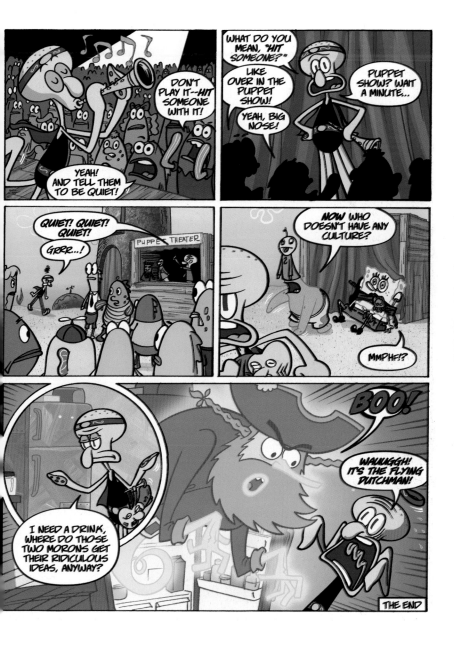

STORY BY JAY LENDER · PENCILS BY GREGG SHIGIEL · INKS BY JEFF ALBRECHT · COLOR BY SNO CONE STUDIOS · LETTERS BY COMICRAFT

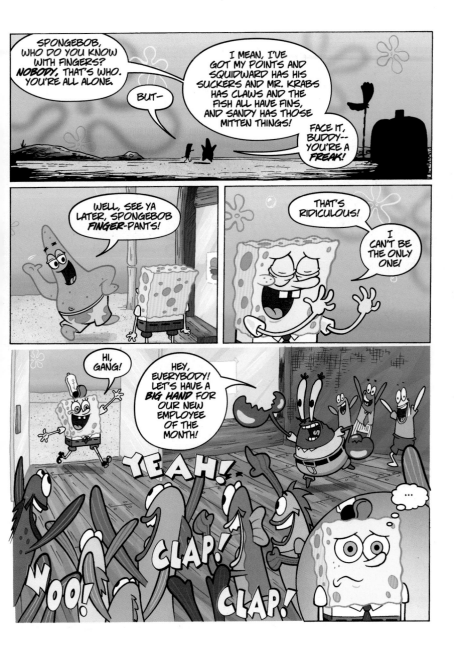

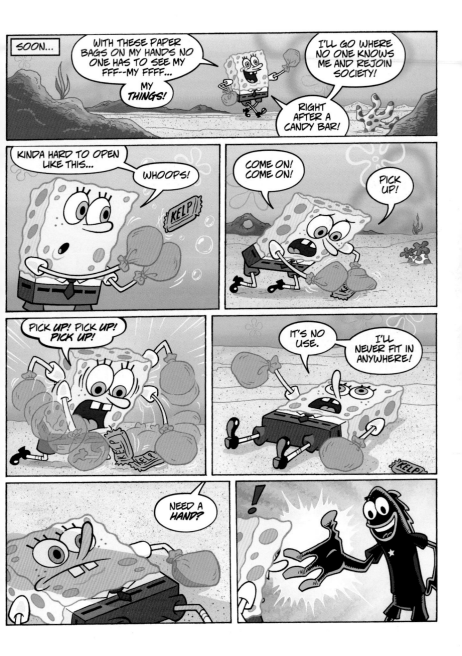

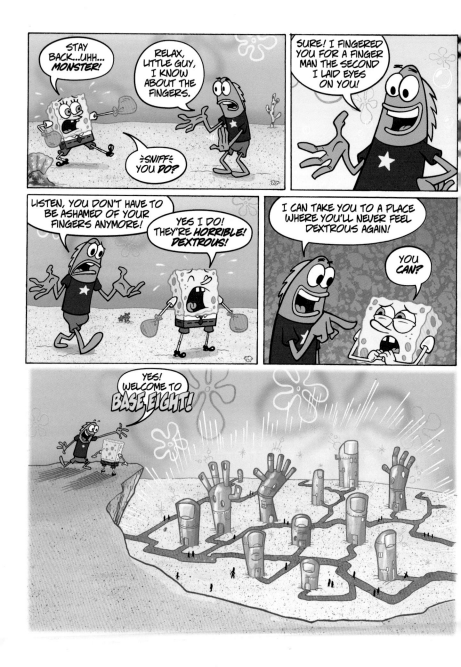

the end.

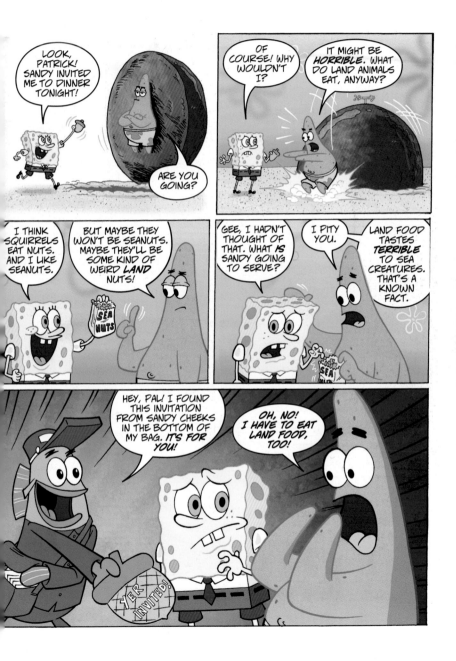

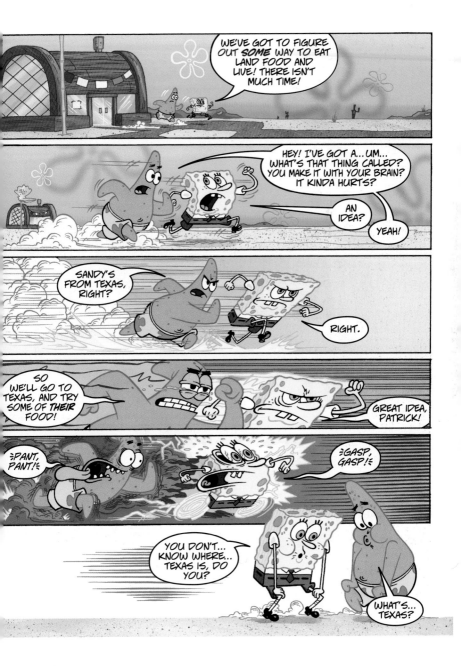

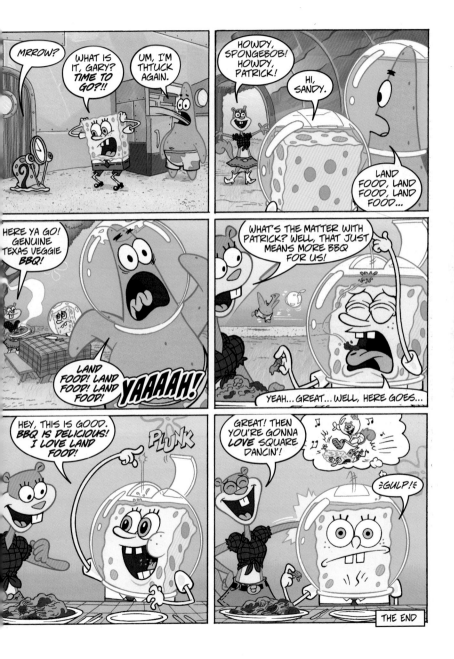

THE END

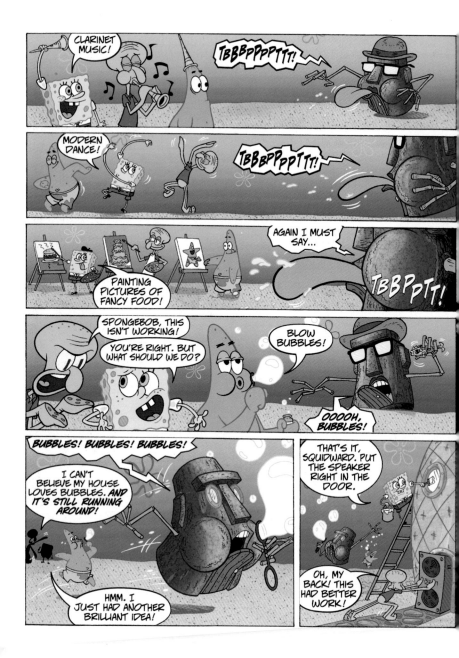

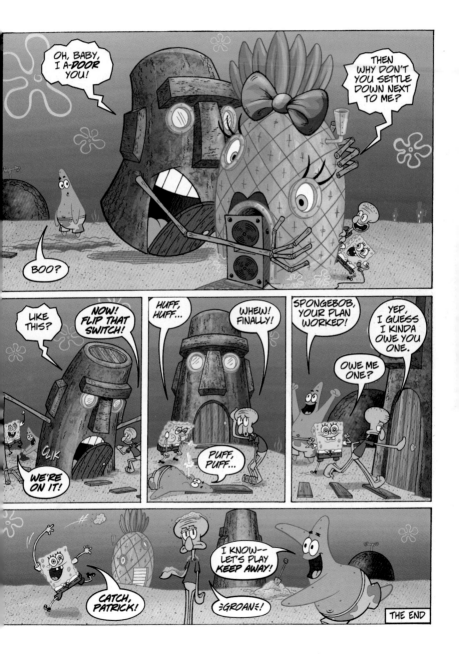

Story: Sam Henderson. Pencils and inks: Vince Deporter. Coloring: Stu Chaifetz. *SpongeBob SquarePants* created by Stephen Hillenburg.

GRAB YOUR SQUAREPANTS!

THE OFFICIAL COMIC AT NEWSAGENTS NOW

Subscriptions: ☎ 0870 428 8214 or visit
www.titanmagazines.co.uk